50 Japanese Home Cooking Recipes for Home

By: Kelly Johnson

Table of Contents

- Tonkatsu (Breaded Pork Cutlet)
- Ramen (Noodle Soup)
- Sukiyaki (Hot Pot)
- Okonomiyaki (Savory Pancake)
- Teriyaki Chicken
- Miso Soup
- Yakitori (Grilled Chicken Skewers)
- Gyoza (Dumplings)
- Nasu Dengaku (Miso-Glazed Eggplant)
- Chirashi Sushi (Scattered Sushi)
- Onigiri (Rice Balls)
- Katsudon (Pork Cutlet Rice Bowl)
- Udon Noodles
- Shabu-Shabu (Hot Pot)
- Tamagoyaki (Japanese Omelette)
- Nikujaga (Meat and Potato Stew)
- Soba Noodles
- Chawanmushi (Savory Egg Custard)
- Tofu Dengaku (Miso-Glazed Tofu)
- Korokke (Croquettes)
- Zaru Soba (Cold Soba Noodles)
- Donburi (Rice Bowl Dishes)
- Agedashi Tofu (Fried Tofu in Broth)
- Ramen Salad
- Takoyaki (Octopus Balls)
- Kinpira Gobo (Braised Burdock Root)
- Shiso Leaf Salad
- Noodle Salad
- Yaki Udon (Fried Udon)
- Miso-Glazed Salmon
- Shimeji Mushroom Stir-Fry
- Spicy Tuna Roll
- Katsu Curry (Curry with Pork Cutlet)
- Spinach Ohitashi (Chilled Spinach)
- Teriyaki Salmon

- Tofu Stir-Fry
- Bento Box (Lunch Box)
- Daikon Salad
- Salmon Rice Balls
- Tori Soba (Chicken Soba)
- Sweet Potato Tempura
- Nasu Udon (Eggplant Udon)
- Dashi Stock
- Goya Champuru (Bitter Melon Stir-Fry)
- Yudofu (Hot Pot Tofu)
- Shio Ramen (Salt Ramen)
- Ebi Furai (Fried Shrimp)
- Pickled Vegetables (Tsukemono)
- Japanese Curry Rice
- Mochi (Rice Cake)

Tonkatsu (Breaded Pork Cutlet)

Ingredients:

- 1 lb pork loin, cut into cutlets
- Salt and pepper, to taste
- 1/2 cup flour
- 1 egg, beaten
- 1 cup panko breadcrumbs
- Oil, for frying
- Tonkatsu sauce, for serving

Instructions:

1. Season pork cutlets with salt and pepper.
2. Dredge each cutlet in flour, dip in beaten egg, then coat with panko breadcrumbs.
3. Heat oil in a pan over medium heat and fry cutlets until golden brown on both sides.
4. Drain on paper towels and serve with tonkatsu sauce.

Ramen (Noodle Soup)

Ingredients:

- 4 cups chicken or pork broth
- 2 servings ramen noodles
- 2 boiled eggs, halved
- 1 cup sliced green onions
- 1 cup sliced mushrooms
- Soy sauce, to taste
- Nori (seaweed), for garnish

Instructions:

1. Cook ramen noodles according to package instructions; drain.
2. In a pot, heat broth and add mushrooms and soy sauce.
3. Divide cooked noodles into bowls, pour hot broth over them, and top with boiled eggs, green onions, and nori.

Sukiyaki (Hot Pot)

Ingredients:

- 1 lb thinly sliced beef
- 1 cup shiitake mushrooms
- 1 cup tofu, cubed
- 1 cup napa cabbage, chopped
- 1 cup udon noodles
- 1/4 cup soy sauce
- 1/4 cup mirin
- 1/4 cup sugar

Instructions:

1. In a hot pot or large skillet, combine soy sauce, mirin, and sugar; bring to a simmer.
2. Add beef, mushrooms, tofu, cabbage, and udon noodles; cook until ingredients are tender.
3. Serve hot, optionally with raw egg for dipping.

Okonomiyaki (Savory Pancake)

Ingredients:

- 2 cups shredded cabbage
- 1 cup flour
- 1/2 cup dashi or water
- 2 eggs
- 1/2 cup sliced green onions
- Oil, for frying
- Okonomiyaki sauce and mayonnaise, for serving

Instructions:

1. In a bowl, mix cabbage, flour, dashi, eggs, and green onions until combined.
2. Heat oil in a skillet and pour in batter to form a pancake.
3. Cook until golden brown on both sides.
4. Serve topped with okonomiyaki sauce and mayonnaise.

Teriyaki Chicken

Ingredients:

- 1 lb chicken thighs, boneless
- 1/4 cup soy sauce
- 1/4 cup mirin
- 2 tbsp sugar
- 1 tbsp sesame seeds (optional)

Instructions:

1. In a bowl, mix soy sauce, mirin, and sugar.
2. Marinate chicken in the sauce for at least 30 minutes.
3. Grill or pan-fry chicken until cooked through, basting with marinade.
4. Sprinkle with sesame seeds before serving.

Miso Soup

Ingredients:

- 4 cups dashi broth
- 3-4 tbsp miso paste
- 1 cup tofu, cubed
- 1/4 cup green onions, sliced
- Seaweed (wakame), optional

Instructions:

1. Heat dashi broth in a pot.
2. Dissolve miso paste in a small amount of hot broth, then stir back into the pot.
3. Add tofu and seaweed; heat gently.
4. Serve garnished with green onions.

Yakitori (Grilled Chicken Skewers)

Ingredients:

- 1 lb chicken thighs, cut into bite-sized pieces
- 1/4 cup soy sauce
- 1/4 cup mirin
- 2 tbsp sake
- 2 tbsp sugar
- Skewers

Instructions:

1. Soak skewers in water for 30 minutes.
2. In a bowl, mix soy sauce, mirin, sake, and sugar to create a marinade.
3. Thread chicken onto skewers and marinate for 30 minutes.
4. Grill skewers over medium heat, basting with marinade, until cooked through.

Gyoza (Dumplings)

Ingredients:

- 1 lb ground pork or chicken
- 1 cup cabbage, finely chopped
- 2 green onions, chopped
- 2 cloves garlic, minced
- 1 tbsp soy sauce
- 1 pack gyoza wrappers
- Oil, for frying

Instructions:

1. In a bowl, combine meat, cabbage, green onions, garlic, and soy sauce.
2. Place a small amount of filling in each wrapper, fold and seal.
3. Heat oil in a pan and fry gyoza until golden brown.
4. Add a splash of water, cover, and steam for a few minutes until cooked through.

Enjoy your cooking!

Nasu Dengaku (Miso-Glazed Eggplant)

Ingredients:

- 2 medium eggplants, halved
- 1/4 cup miso paste
- 2 tbsp sugar
- 2 tbsp mirin
- 1 tbsp sake
- Sesame seeds and green onions, for garnish

Instructions:

1. Preheat the oven to 400°F (200°C).
2. Score the cut sides of the eggplants and brush with oil. Place them cut-side up on a baking sheet.
3. In a bowl, mix miso paste, sugar, mirin, and sake until smooth.
4. Spread the miso mixture over the cut sides of the eggplants.
5. Bake for 20-25 minutes until eggplants are tender and caramelized. Garnish with sesame seeds and green onions before serving.

Chirashi Sushi (Scattered Sushi)

Ingredients:

- 2 cups sushi rice
- 2 1/2 cups water
- 1/4 cup rice vinegar
- 2 tbsp sugar
- 1 tsp salt
- Assorted toppings (sliced raw fish, vegetables, egg, seaweed)

Instructions:

1. Rinse sushi rice under cold water until water runs clear; cook with water in a rice cooker.
2. In a small saucepan, heat rice vinegar, sugar, and salt until dissolved.
3. Once rice is cooked, transfer to a bowl and mix in the vinegar mixture. Let cool.
4. Spread rice on a serving platter and arrange assorted toppings on top.

Onigiri (Rice Balls)

Ingredients:

- 2 cups sushi rice
- 2 1/2 cups water
- Salt, to taste
- Nori (seaweed), cut into strips
- Fillings (pickled plum, salmon, or tuna)

Instructions:

1. Rinse sushi rice under cold water and cook with water in a rice cooker.
2. Once cooked, let cool slightly; season with salt.
3. With wet hands, take a small amount of rice and flatten it. Place a filling in the center and mold the rice into a triangle or ball shape.
4. Wrap with a strip of nori before serving.

Katsudon (Pork Cutlet Rice Bowl)

Ingredients:

- 1 lb pork loin, cut into cutlets
- Salt and pepper, to taste
- 1/2 cup flour
- 1 egg, beaten
- 1 cup panko breadcrumbs
- 2 cups cooked rice
- 2 eggs (for the sauce)
- 1/4 cup dashi broth
- 2 tbsp soy sauce
- 1 tbsp mirin
- Green onions, for garnish

Instructions:

1. Season pork cutlets with salt and pepper, then dredge in flour, dip in egg, and coat with panko.
2. Fry cutlets in oil until golden brown, then slice into strips.
3. In a pan, combine dashi broth, soy sauce, and mirin; bring to a simmer.
4. Add cutlets, pour beaten eggs over, and cover until eggs are set.
5. Serve over rice and garnish with green onions.

Udon Noodles

Ingredients:

- 2 cups udon noodles
- 4 cups dashi broth
- 2 green onions, chopped
- Soy sauce, to taste
- Toppings (tempura, mushrooms, etc.)

Instructions:

1. Cook udon noodles according to package instructions; drain.
2. In a pot, heat dashi broth and add soy sauce to taste.
3. Divide cooked noodles into bowls and pour hot broth over them.
4. Top with green onions and any additional toppings before serving.

Shabu-Shabu (Hot Pot)

Ingredients:

- 1 lb thinly sliced beef
- 4 cups dashi broth
- Assorted vegetables (napa cabbage, mushrooms, tofu)
- Dipping sauces (ponzu or sesame sauce)

Instructions:

1. Heat dashi broth in a large pot.
2. Arrange sliced beef and vegetables on a platter.
3. Dip beef and vegetables into the hot broth until cooked; serve with dipping sauces.

Tamagoyaki (Japanese Omelette)

Ingredients:

- 4 eggs
- 1 tbsp sugar
- 1 tbsp soy sauce
- 1 tbsp mirin
- Oil, for cooking

Instructions:

1. In a bowl, whisk together eggs, sugar, soy sauce, and mirin.
2. Heat a rectangular pan and lightly oil it.
3. Pour a thin layer of egg mixture; cook until just set, then roll it to one side of the pan.
4. Add another layer of egg mixture, lifting the rolled omelette to let uncooked egg flow underneath.
5. Repeat until all the egg is used; slice and serve.

Nikujaga (Meat and Potato Stew)

Ingredients:

- 1 lb thinly sliced beef
- 2 potatoes, peeled and diced
- 1 onion, sliced
- 2 carrots, sliced
- 1/4 cup soy sauce
- 1/4 cup mirin
- 1/4 cup sugar
- 2 cups dashi broth

Instructions:

1. In a pot, sauté onions until translucent.
2. Add beef and cook until browned.
3. Add potatoes, carrots, dashi broth, soy sauce, mirin, and sugar.
4. Simmer until vegetables are tender and flavors meld. Serve warm.

Enjoy your cooking!

Soba Noodles

Ingredients:

- 8 oz soba noodles
- Water, for boiling
- Soy sauce or dipping sauce, for serving

Instructions:

1. Bring a pot of water to a boil.
2. Add soba noodles and cook according to package instructions (usually 4-5 minutes).
3. Drain and rinse under cold water to stop cooking.
4. Serve chilled with soy sauce or your choice of dipping sauce.

Chawanmushi (Savory Egg Custard)

Ingredients:

- 4 eggs
- 2 cups dashi broth
- 2 tbsp soy sauce
- 1 tbsp mirin
- 1/4 cup sliced mushrooms
- 1/4 cup cooked shrimp or chicken (optional)
- Chopped green onions, for garnish

Instructions:

1. In a bowl, whisk together eggs, dashi broth, soy sauce, and mirin.
2. Strain the mixture into a measuring cup to remove bubbles.
3. Divide mushrooms and shrimp (if using) into small cups and pour the egg mixture on top.
4. Steam in a steamer or pot with a lid for about 15-20 minutes, until set.
5. Garnish with green onions before serving.

Tofu Dengaku (Miso-Glazed Tofu)

Ingredients:

- 1 block firm tofu, sliced
- 1/4 cup miso paste
- 2 tbsp sugar
- 2 tbsp mirin
- 1 tbsp sake
- Sesame seeds and green onions, for garnish

Instructions:

1. Preheat the oven to 400°F (200°C).
2. Pat tofu dry and place on a baking sheet.
3. In a bowl, mix miso paste, sugar, mirin, and sake until smooth.
4. Spread the miso mixture over the tofu slices.
5. Bake for 20-25 minutes until golden and slightly caramelized. Garnish with sesame seeds and green onions.

Korokke (Croquettes)

Ingredients:

- 2 medium potatoes, peeled and cubed
- 1/2 cup ground meat (beef or pork)
- 1/4 onion, finely chopped
- Salt and pepper, to taste
- 1/2 cup flour
- 1 egg, beaten
- 1 cup panko breadcrumbs
- Oil, for frying

Instructions:

1. Boil potatoes until tender; mash and set aside.
2. In a pan, sauté onions until translucent, then add ground meat; cook until browned.
3. Mix meat and onions into mashed potatoes; season with salt and pepper.
4. Form mixture into patties, then dredge in flour, dip in egg, and coat with panko.
5. Fry in hot oil until golden brown on both sides; drain on paper towels before serving.

Zaru Soba (Cold Soba Noodles)

Ingredients:

- 8 oz soba noodles
- 1/4 cup soy sauce
- 1 tbsp wasabi (optional)
- Sliced green onions, for garnish

Instructions:

1. Boil soba noodles according to package instructions, then drain and rinse under cold water.
2. Serve noodles on a bamboo mat or plate.
3. Mix soy sauce with wasabi (if using) and serve as a dipping sauce. Garnish with green onions.

Donburi (Rice Bowl Dishes)

Ingredients:

- 2 cups cooked rice
- 1 lb protein (chicken, beef, or tofu)
- 1 cup vegetables (carrots, peas, etc.)
- 1/4 cup soy sauce
- 2 tbsp mirin
- 1 tbsp sugar

Instructions:

1. Cook protein in a pan and add vegetables; stir-fry until tender.
2. Add soy sauce, mirin, and sugar; simmer for a few minutes.
3. Serve over a bowl of warm rice.

Agedashi Tofu (Fried Tofu in Broth)

Ingredients:

- 1 block firm tofu, cut into cubes
- 1/4 cup cornstarch
- Oil, for frying
- 2 cups dashi broth
- 2 tbsp soy sauce
- 1 tbsp mirin
- Grated daikon and green onions, for garnish

Instructions:

1. Coat tofu cubes in cornstarch.
2. Heat oil in a pan and fry tofu until golden brown; drain on paper towels.
3. In a pot, heat dashi broth, soy sauce, and mirin.
4. Serve tofu in the broth, garnished with grated daikon and green onions.

Ramen Salad

Ingredients:

- 2 servings ramen noodles
- 1 cup shredded carrots
- 1 cup cucumber, thinly sliced
- 1/4 cup sliced green onions
- 1/4 cup sesame seeds

Dressing:

- 2 tbsp soy sauce
- 1 tbsp rice vinegar
- 1 tbsp sesame oil
- 1 tsp sugar

Instructions:

1. Cook ramen noodles according to package instructions; drain and cool.
2. In a bowl, combine cooked noodles, carrots, cucumber, green onions, and sesame seeds.
3. In a separate bowl, whisk together dressing ingredients; pour over the salad and toss to combine.

Enjoy your cooking!

Takoyaki (Octopus Balls)

Ingredients:

- 1 cup takoyaki flour (or all-purpose flour)
- 1 1/2 cups dashi broth
- 1 egg
- 1 cup cooked octopus, diced
- 1/2 cup green onions, chopped
- 1/2 cup pickled ginger, chopped
- Oil, for cooking
- Takoyaki sauce and bonito flakes, for serving

Instructions:

1. In a bowl, mix takoyaki flour, dashi broth, and egg until smooth.
2. Preheat a takoyaki pan and lightly oil each hole.
3. Pour batter into the holes, filling them halfway.
4. Add diced octopus, green onions, and pickled ginger into each hole.
5. Pour more batter on top and cook until golden brown, turning with a skewer.
6. Serve with takoyaki sauce and bonito flakes.

Kinpira Gobo (Braised Burdock Root)

Ingredients:

- 1 burdock root, julienned
- 1 carrot, julienned
- 2 tbsp soy sauce
- 1 tbsp mirin
- 1 tbsp sugar
- 1 tbsp sesame oil
- Sesame seeds, for garnish

Instructions:

1. Heat sesame oil in a pan and add burdock root and carrot; stir-fry for a few minutes.
2. Add soy sauce, mirin, and sugar; cook until vegetables are tender and the liquid has evaporated.
3. Garnish with sesame seeds before serving.

Shiso Leaf Salad

Ingredients:

- 1 bunch shiso leaves, washed and dried
- 1 cucumber, thinly sliced
- 1 cup cherry tomatoes, halved
- 1/4 cup rice vinegar
- 1 tbsp soy sauce
- 1 tsp sugar

Instructions:

1. In a bowl, combine rice vinegar, soy sauce, and sugar to make the dressing.
2. In a serving bowl, layer shiso leaves, cucumber, and cherry tomatoes.
3. Drizzle with dressing and toss gently before serving.

Noodle Salad

Ingredients:

- 8 oz cooked soba or udon noodles
- 1 cup shredded carrots
- 1 cup bell pepper, thinly sliced
- 1/4 cup sliced green onions
- 1/4 cup sesame dressing

Instructions:

1. In a large bowl, combine cooked noodles, carrots, bell pepper, and green onions.
2. Drizzle with sesame dressing and toss to combine. Serve chilled.

Yaki Udon (Fried Udon)

Ingredients:

- 8 oz udon noodles
- 1 cup sliced vegetables (carrots, bell peppers, cabbage)
- 1/2 cup sliced protein (chicken, beef, or tofu)
- 2 tbsp soy sauce
- 1 tbsp oyster sauce (optional)
- Oil, for frying

Instructions:

1. Cook udon noodles according to package instructions; drain.
2. Heat oil in a pan and stir-fry protein until cooked; add vegetables and cook until tender.
3. Add cooked udon noodles, soy sauce, and oyster sauce; toss to combine and heat through.

Miso-Glazed Salmon

Ingredients:

- 2 salmon fillets
- 1/4 cup miso paste
- 2 tbsp mirin
- 1 tbsp sugar
- Sesame seeds, for garnish

Instructions:

1. Preheat the oven to 400°F (200°C).
2. In a bowl, mix miso paste, mirin, and sugar to create a glaze.
3. Coat salmon fillets with the glaze and place on a baking sheet.
4. Bake for 12-15 minutes until salmon is cooked through. Garnish with sesame seeds before serving.

Shimeji Mushroom Stir-Fry

Ingredients:

- 200g shimeji mushrooms, trimmed
- 1 bell pepper, sliced
- 1 carrot, julienned
- 2 tbsp soy sauce
- 1 tbsp sesame oil
- 1 clove garlic, minced

Instructions:

1. Heat sesame oil in a pan and sauté garlic until fragrant.
2. Add shimeji mushrooms, bell pepper, and carrot; stir-fry for a few minutes.
3. Add soy sauce and cook until vegetables are tender. Serve hot.

Spicy Tuna Roll

Ingredients:

- 1 cup sushi rice, cooked
- 1/2 lb sushi-grade tuna, diced
- 1 tbsp mayonnaise
- 1 tsp sriracha (or to taste)
- 4 sheets nori (seaweed)
- Soy sauce, for serving

Instructions:

1. In a bowl, mix diced tuna with mayonnaise and sriracha.
2. Lay a sheet of nori on a bamboo mat and spread a thin layer of sushi rice on top.
3. Place a line of the tuna mixture in the center and roll tightly.
4. Slice into pieces and serve with soy sauce.

Enjoy your cooking!

Katsu Curry (Curry with Pork Cutlet)

Ingredients:

- 1 lb pork loin, cut into cutlets
- Salt and pepper, to taste
- 1/2 cup flour
- 1 egg, beaten
- 1 cup panko breadcrumbs
- Oil, for frying
- 2 cups curry roux (store-bought or homemade)
- 2 cups water
- 2 cups cooked rice

Instructions:

1. Season pork cutlets with salt and pepper. Dredge in flour, dip in egg, and coat with panko.
2. Heat oil in a pan and fry cutlets until golden brown; drain on paper towels.
3. In a pot, mix curry roux and water; cook until thickened.
4. Serve sliced katsu over rice, topped with curry sauce.

Spinach Ohitashi (Chilled Spinach)

Ingredients:

- 1 bunch fresh spinach
- 1/4 cup soy sauce
- 1 tbsp mirin
- Bonito flakes (optional)

Instructions:

1. Blanch spinach in boiling water for 1-2 minutes; drain and rinse with cold water.
2. Squeeze out excess water and cut into bite-sized pieces.
3. In a bowl, mix soy sauce and mirin; pour over spinach.
4. Serve chilled, topped with bonito flakes if desired.

Teriyaki Salmon

Ingredients:

- 2 salmon fillets
- 1/4 cup soy sauce
- 2 tbsp mirin
- 1 tbsp sugar
- Sesame seeds, for garnish
- Green onions, chopped, for garnish

Instructions:

1. In a bowl, mix soy sauce, mirin, and sugar to create the marinade.
2. Marinate salmon fillets for at least 30 minutes.
3. Heat a pan over medium heat and cook salmon skin-side down for about 4-5 minutes; flip and cook for another 2-3 minutes, brushing with marinade.
4. Serve garnished with sesame seeds and green onions.

Tofu Stir-Fry

Ingredients:

- 1 block firm tofu, cubed
- 2 cups mixed vegetables (bell peppers, broccoli, carrots)
- 2 tbsp soy sauce
- 1 tbsp sesame oil
- 2 cloves garlic, minced

Instructions:

1. Heat sesame oil in a pan and sauté garlic until fragrant.
2. Add tofu and cook until golden brown on all sides.
3. Add mixed vegetables and soy sauce; stir-fry until vegetables are tender. Serve hot.

Bento Box (Lunch Box)

Ingredients:

- Cooked rice
- Protein (grilled chicken, teriyaki salmon, or tofu)
- Pickled vegetables (like pickled radish)
- Chilled salad (like cucumber or seaweed salad)
- Fruit (like sliced apple or grapes)

Instructions:

1. In a bento box, neatly compartmentalize cooked rice, protein, pickled vegetables, salad, and fruit.
2. Garnish as desired and pack for lunch.

Daikon Salad

Ingredients:

- 1 small daikon radish, peeled and grated
- 1 carrot, grated
- 2 tbsp rice vinegar
- 1 tbsp soy sauce
- 1 tsp sugar
- Sesame seeds, for garnish

Instructions:

1. In a bowl, combine grated daikon and carrot.
2. In a separate bowl, whisk together rice vinegar, soy sauce, and sugar.
3. Pour dressing over the salad and toss to combine.
4. Serve garnished with sesame seeds.

Salmon Rice Balls

Ingredients:

- 2 cups cooked sushi rice
- 1/2 cup cooked salmon, flaked
- 1 tbsp soy sauce
- 1/2 tsp wasabi (optional)
- Nori (seaweed), cut into strips

Instructions:

1. In a bowl, mix cooked rice with flaked salmon, soy sauce, and wasabi (if using).
2. With wet hands, shape the mixture into balls or triangles.
3. Wrap with strips of nori before serving.

Tori Soba (Chicken Soba)

Ingredients:

- 8 oz soba noodles
- 1 cup cooked chicken, shredded
- 2 cups chicken broth
- 1/4 cup soy sauce
- 1/4 cup green onions, sliced
- Vegetables (carrots, spinach)

Instructions:

1. Cook soba noodles according to package instructions; drain.
2. In a pot, heat chicken broth and soy sauce; add shredded chicken and vegetables; simmer until heated through.
3. Serve soba noodles in bowls and ladle broth with chicken and vegetables over the top. Garnish with green onions.

Enjoy your cooking!

Sweet Potato Tempura

Ingredients:

- 1 medium sweet potato, peeled and sliced into thin rounds
- 1 cup tempura batter mix (or 1 cup all-purpose flour and 1/2 cup cold water)
- Oil, for frying
- Sea salt, for serving

Instructions:

1. Heat oil in a deep pan to 350°F (175°C).
2. In a bowl, mix tempura batter according to package instructions (or combine flour and water until smooth).
3. Dip sweet potato slices into the batter and carefully place them in the hot oil.
4. Fry until golden brown and crispy, about 3-4 minutes.
5. Remove and drain on paper towels; sprinkle with sea salt before serving.

Nasu Udon (Eggplant Udon)

Ingredients:

- 8 oz udon noodles
- 1 medium eggplant, cut into bite-sized pieces
- 2 tbsp soy sauce
- 1 tbsp mirin
- 1 cup dashi broth
- 1 tbsp sesame oil
- Green onions, sliced, for garnish

Instructions:

1. Cook udon noodles according to package instructions; drain and set aside.
2. In a pan, heat sesame oil and sauté eggplant until tender.
3. Add dashi broth, soy sauce, and mirin; bring to a simmer.
4. Add cooked udon noodles to the broth and heat through.
5. Serve garnished with green onions.

Dashi Stock

Ingredients:

- 4 cups water
- 1 piece kombu (dried kelp), about 4 inches
- 1 cup bonito flakes

Instructions:

1. In a pot, soak kombu in water for about 30 minutes.
2. Heat the water with kombu over medium heat until just before boiling; remove kombu.
3. Add bonito flakes and simmer for about 5 minutes.
4. Strain the stock through a fine sieve or cheesecloth. Use immediately or store in the fridge for up to a week.

Goya Champuru (Bitter Melon Stir-Fry)

Ingredients:

- 1 medium goya (bitter melon), sliced
- 1/2 lb firm tofu, cubed
- 1/2 lb pork or chicken, thinly sliced (optional)
- 2 tbsp soy sauce
- 1 tbsp mirin
- 1 tbsp sesame oil
- 1 clove garlic, minced

Instructions:

1. Heat sesame oil in a pan and sauté garlic until fragrant.
2. Add pork or chicken (if using) and cook until browned.
3. Add tofu and cook until golden.
4. Stir in sliced goya and cook for about 3-4 minutes until tender.
5. Add soy sauce and mirin; stir to combine and serve hot.

Yudofu (Hot Pot Tofu)

Ingredients:

- 1 block silken tofu, cut into cubes
- 4 cups dashi broth
- 2 tbsp soy sauce
- 1 tbsp mirin
- Green onions, chopped, for garnish
- Grated daikon, for serving (optional)

Instructions:

1. In a pot, heat dashi broth and add soy sauce and mirin.
2. Gently add tofu cubes and simmer for about 5-7 minutes until heated through.
3. Serve hot, garnished with green onions and grated daikon if desired.

Shio Ramen (Salt Ramen)

Ingredients:

- 4 cups chicken or pork broth
- 2 tbsp soy sauce
- 1 tbsp miso (optional)
- 8 oz ramen noodles
- Toppings: sliced chashu pork, soft-boiled eggs, green onions, nori, and bamboo shoots

Instructions:

1. In a pot, heat broth and add soy sauce and miso (if using).
2. Cook ramen noodles according to package instructions; drain.
3. Divide noodles into bowls and ladle hot broth over them.
4. Top with chashu pork, soft-boiled eggs, green onions, nori, and bamboo shoots before serving.

Enjoy your cooking!

Ebi Furai (Fried Shrimp)

Ingredients:

- 1 lb large shrimp, peeled and deveined
- Salt and pepper, to taste
- 1/2 cup flour
- 1 egg, beaten
- 1 cup panko breadcrumbs
- Oil, for frying
- Tonkatsu sauce, for serving

Instructions:

1. Season shrimp with salt and pepper.
2. Dredge each shrimp in flour, dip in beaten egg, and coat with panko breadcrumbs.
3. Heat oil in a deep pan to 350°F (175°C).
4. Fry shrimp until golden brown, about 2-3 minutes.
5. Drain on paper towels and serve with tonkatsu sauce.

Pickled Vegetables (Tsukemono)

Ingredients:

- 1 cucumber, thinly sliced
- 1 carrot, julienned
- 1 radish, thinly sliced
- 1/4 cup rice vinegar
- 1 tbsp sugar
- 1 tsp salt

Instructions:

1. In a bowl, mix rice vinegar, sugar, and salt until dissolved.
2. Add cucumber, carrot, and radish; mix well.
3. Let sit for at least 30 minutes in the refrigerator before serving.

Japanese Curry Rice

Ingredients:

- 1 lb meat (chicken, beef, or pork), diced
- 1 onion, chopped
- 2 carrots, diced
- 2 potatoes, diced
- 4 cups water
- 1 box Japanese curry roux (e.g., Golden Curry)
- Cooked rice, for serving

Instructions:

1. In a pot, sauté onion until translucent.
2. Add meat and cook until browned.
3. Add carrots and potatoes, then pour in water; bring to a boil.
4. Reduce heat and simmer until vegetables are tender.
5. Break up the curry roux into the pot and stir until dissolved; cook for an additional 10 minutes.
6. Serve curry over cooked rice.

Mochi (Rice Cake)

Ingredients:

- 1 cup sweet rice flour (mochi flour)
- 1/4 cup sugar
- 1 cup water
- Cornstarch or potato starch, for dusting

Instructions:

1. In a microwave-safe bowl, mix sweet rice flour, sugar, and water until smooth.
2. Cover the bowl with plastic wrap and microwave for 1 minute. Stir, then microwave for another minute. Stir again, and microwave for an additional 30 seconds.
3. Dust a surface with cornstarch or potato starch. Turn the mochi mixture onto the surface and dust the top.
4. Once cool, cut into pieces or shape as desired.

Enjoy your cooking!